London to Moscow:
our route in red

Acknowledgements

With thanks to my parents, Ann and Peter and to the special encouragement of the writer, Tahir Shah[1].
From his work I first learned the need for "courage to climb".

This book originates in a blog I wrote as we travelled. You can reach me with comments at
JJTinklepaugh@gmail.com

Anxiety

Have been browsing for wheelchair travellers' experiences: "James Ballardie is a wheelchair user who has been travelling the world without planning an accessible path through it. And it was all going pretty well until he reached China. 'Take crossing the road, for example. Even on back streets it could mean life or death. These cities have the most aggressive driving culture I've ever seen. Most pedestrians cross roads in swarms, presumably on the basis that it's safer in numbers. It's difficult to see where wheelchairs can successfully fit into the scrum. So why not wait and cross the road at a quieter section with less risk of collision? There's a good reason. Most main roads in Chinese cities are lined with big iron fences that are impossible to climb over so pedestrians have no choice but to use the footbridges and subways which mostly have stairs. Those that have lifts tend either to be broken or only operable with a key which I was unable to find anywhere' " [2].

Never to be able to cross a road in China. Pavements fenced off from the roads, massed with pedestrians, occasional barriers across the pavement to keep out cyclists. Only way over the road is by bridge, up steep stairs. No other wheelchairs to be seen.

I must stop looking at other people's postings.

London St Pancras: Monday

There are journeys, a movement from one point to the other which with repetition that can become indistinct; then there are expeditions. This can accurately be described in that way, travelling by train to explore Asia, a continent new for us. Years and months of planning for an event that seemed moored in a static unreachable future, that event now has us in its grip.

Planning this, why so difficult? Partly because all the journey segments are so interdependent; need booked travel to and from China before applying for Chinese visa, which requires Trans Sib tickets, which need Russian visa, which needs train to Moscow, which needs Belarus visa, which needs train tickets… Unlocking the Trans Siberian segment was the key (can a lock be the key?)

For the Trans Sib we really needed a wheelchair friendly space: was such a thing possible? Answer took months of enquiry and submission of documents to Russian Railways (via RealRussia[3]). Documentary proof of disability required, but the UK Government doesn't provide it. Forms from the DWP, letters from my GP and from my imagination were sent and weren't sufficient. Eventually, as we were starting to rethink the whole trip, RealRussia told us they had tickets for a disabled compartment in their Moscow office. The tickets don't mention disability: two second class berths is all they say. Midnight Saturday will show us whether we can get on the train.

So many operators to deal with. Eurostar for this stretch, Deutsches Bahn for Brussels to Cologne and then the overnight to Warsaw; Polrail to continue to Moscow, Russian Railways for trans Manchurian to Beijing, Chinese Railway agencies for continuing through Xi'an, Shanghai, Hong Kong.

Are the stations accessible? Brought up on rail terminals being at ground level, I have to force my imagination to picture vast structures built over several stories connected by steep pyramids of stairs. And then I remember Riga station, an old Soviet structure, flights of stairs (why 'flights'), lofty platforms inaccessible to us; with one exception, a single lift which fortunately led to our platform (getting on the train itself was another story, made happy by the kindness of a stranger)

Jordan airlines to take us back through Bangkok and Amman. Even there weeks and many phone calls and emails to get acknowledgement that we need assistance. At least the conversation was possible.[4]

We did not find a way to have that conversation with Russian Railways.
CTS on behalf of China said no assistance is possible. No argument.

Brussels Midi station

Reaching Bruxelles an enveloping heat hits us as we leave the station. We have two hours to wander the streets. Men, largely West African, hang around. We are struck by the lack of smiling.

Further into smaller streets of poorly maintained 19th century houses, shops, we see mostly Arab looking men and women Syrian?

We come across no grand buildings, none of the civic squares which I remember from our previous trip inter-railing round Europe 16 years ago.

A Slavic looking man, bald and podgy and perhaps drunk, comes up to us mistaking our answer of "the UK" in response to "Where are you from?" as "the Ukraine". He reaches out a hand to shake. I am wary; as a wheelchair user I am a sitting target, my private space can be regarded as most definitely public. Nevertheless I don't like to be too impolite and we end up brushing fingers.

We wander slowly back to the station.

18.27 train to Cologne

We wait. Time has stopped. The space is crowded, airless.

An unkempt man arrives and takes us up in a lift to a platform blocked with groups and their luggage heaps. The train is there but the doors are locked. The clock ticks, door opens and the scrum pushes.

Our attendant holds his ground with the wheelchair ramp and we are in ahead of the horde.

The train sets off many people still looking for seats, barricading aisles with their belongings.

After leaving suburban Bruxelles we come to a halt, a train has broken down in front of us.

For a while the train idles along, then picks up speed.

The late evening shoots occasional glances through the trees.

We reach Koln.

It is dark and the rain is falling in sheets. We walk every so often to the station exit to glimpse the cathedral imposing itself against a velvet sky, the station far livelier and brighter ushering in people with umbrellas and macs dripping. We don't have any wet weather gear. In fact we have little of anything as all we have must fit into the small bag on the back of my chair or in the rucksack that Peter carries; he needs his hands free to push my chair.[5]

We go to the information booth to ask for help. The woman is cheerful, reassuring, though the train is running late due to technical difficulties.

We should go wait on the platform near the middle, and wait for the man in the red cap to help us. We had come across him earlier, dressed in his red cap and dark waistcoat. He brought out a very well-thumbed book detailing every train and carriage, showing where you board.

So well ordered.

Overnight to Warsaw:

The platform is dimly lit. The train very high off the ground, the ramp is placed on a wheelbarrow like contraption with a handle to pull it along and a lever like a bicycle pump to raise it up.

There are just three minutes to get on the train. The conductor shrugs when we ask what we do with the wheelchair in the narrow corridor. No room to turn. In spite of the shrug, the conductor holds out his chubby hands for me to grasp. We leave the chair and with Peter behind me we stagger down the corridor to the cabin. It is narrow with two bunks and a wash basin. The toilet is way down the narrow corridor, so going there demands effort, moving feet whilst remaining upright.

The wheelchair cannot stay near the conductor's booth, so Peter goes back to fold it and fit into the cabin somehow.

The train departs and our carriage sways violently. Standing up at the washbasin is a challenge; we are both falling about.

I lie on the bottom bunk, feeling every movement. The only way for Peter to climb out of the top bunk is to put his foot on the cupboard.

7 Praha 22:28
Warschau

Suddenly the conductor bangs on the door; it is 10 am and we arrive in Warsaw in ten minutes.

Warsaw: Tuesday

The station that we alight into is underground and dimly lit. We are helped off the train using the same contraption of a ramp mounted on a long wheelbarrow. They ask where we want to go, we say the name of the hotel and they lose interest. The problem is that though the hotel is just across the road, the only way to cross the road is via an underpass with steps at both ends of it, the last flight offering the choice of an escalator or stairs. Security guards awkwardly carry the wheelchair down the steps and up the escalator. The heat is searing, very little breeze, the light blinding. We find a cash point which disgorges zlotys: £20 or £200 worth? - we have no idea.

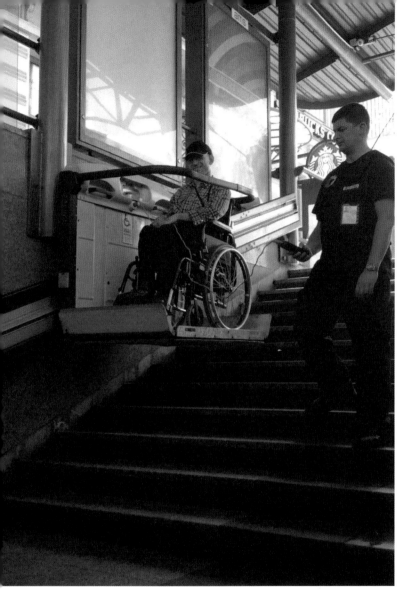

Hotel check in, rest up, and we go off to explore.

We find a stairlift down into the underground city of shops that is part of the labyrinthine subway system we had used earlier – flower stalls, fruit stalls, bakeries with bread the size of bricks and cakes shrivelling under the lights.

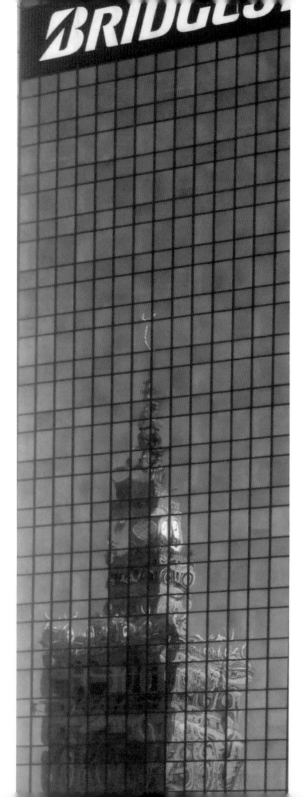

Stalin's gift to Poland, Warsaw's Palace of Culture.

We walk around the old town which was almost entirely rebuilt after the Second World War.

Getting on the Moscow train: Wednesday

We arrive in the station forty minutes early as asked. Time passes. The woman in the information centre makes several calls. Eventually, ten minutes before our train is due to depart, two security guards in their yellow bibs turn up.

One takes the wheelchair and we begin walking. Suddenly he lets go of the handles and wanders off. My chair continues[6].

Another guard wanders over and takes over pushing. They do not seem to know where we are going.

We show the tickets.

Eventually after two lifts and a lot of passageways we are on platform three.

Our carriage is at the far end. The train is getting ready to depart. We dash for the waiting ramp and are shoved on board, the wrong way around, facing into the end of the compartment, no room for the wheelchair to turn or me to get out of it.

Peter and the fat conductor have a disagreement in two languages.

The train is moving.

 Eventually we manage to get help to fold the wheelchair footplates and by manoeuvring in the awkward space, I pull myself out, grabbing onto a convenient handle. The wheelchair is folded and I am helped past it down the narrow corridor.

Our compartment already has two occupants. We squeeze in and I am dumped on a lower berth.

Belorus

The border town, Terespol is signalled by a long delay.

A serious young Polish guard gets on to check passports. A youngish woman with a blond ponytail and green uniform arrives, one of the Belorussians border guards. She asks for passports then squats to my level to stare in my face, then looks at my passport picture with evident disbelief.

Time stands still as we doubt our own identities. She stands at last, takes the passports, leaving transit forms to be filled. Each letter must fit in its own tiny box, not an easy task for a clerk with a steady hand. My writing demands something more expansive.

We notice a large hare wandering down the platform.

The train lurches backwards to a huge workshop with massive overhead gantries and heavy lifting gear. Tired looking men with massive spanners unscrew nuts, remove couplings, the carriage is winched up, the old bogies are removed and new ones slid into place along the dual gauge track. Hard physical labour, and exacting. Are nuts ever not replaced?

Sealed from the labourers by double glazing we feel like spectators in a coal mine. What effort. Would it not be easier to get passengers to switch to carriages with appropriate gauge?

All the while women are knocking on the window holding up cardboard signs offering home-made food. They are desperate to sell in the short time they have.

The train is recoupled, we trundle on.

Moscow Belorussky Station: Thursday

Quite suddenly the train is passing among tall buildings, construction sites, roads.

We scrabble in the compartment re-assembling the wheelchair, doing a jig saw puzzle inside a jig saw puzzle.

The train stops. Peter starts moving rucksack and folded wheelchair, seat and backrest to a now empty compartment nearer the exit. Then, when everyone else has got off, he carries the folded wheelchair off the train. A large audience gathers.

He carries rucksack and wheelchair bag to join the rest of our stuff. Then frog marches me down the corridor, lifts me off the train, into the chair, several guards trying to help but there's no room. My legs go into clonus. He holds them till they quieten. Our bags are loaded on a trolley and we are off into the Moscow sunshine. 27 degrees. Straight out of the station. No steps! Where are we going? Taxi. Two drivers not interested. 1500 roubles. No. We offer 800. No.

The porter takes us out of the station, to the far end of a car park, a friend? Anyway a friendly, well- lived face, an older man with a spacious upright estate car, happy to take us for 800. He has time and gentleness.

Through quite traditional streets, a park runs alongside the road, children's swings. Then major roads, the Kremlin, across the river, via the canals and we are at Bakrushina, the Ibis hotel.

Moscow :Thursday

I do my daily stretches to counteract my spasticity , then step out in the Moscow heat of the day. The Tretyakov area is small scale, quiet roads, easily walkable and clearly an area where people actually live. I see people lining up to buy fruit at a small stall. An old woman leaning on a walking frame puts her hands out in supplication.

Another old woman is leaning by a fence with an apple offering pieces to passers-by.

Some have been left behind in this prosperous area.

We find an Italian restaurant in a courtyard. This area is far from our image of the vast building complexes and nine lane racetrack highways of the larger city.

The very informal courtyard restaurant

We walk through a park.

An old woman in green overalls is bent double weeding the beds.

Bizarre touches abound in this city, where small parks have huge cushions like play areas for adults to loll in; the nearby footbridge has fake trees especially for people to attach 'love padlocks'.

Walking on we reach the Moskvoretsky bridge leading to the Kremlin.

On the bridge is a man guarding hand-written memorials to the assassinated political activist Boris Nemtsov, on the spot where he was killed on 27th February 2015. Nemtsov was a well known critic of the Kremlin. It intrigued us that the authorities allowed in this spot such an open display of dissent from the official truth.

There seems to be an ill-defined area of free expression allowed - as long as it doesn't threaten those in power.

Into Red Square with the Kremlin facing us, we pass the Lenin mausoleum, a windowless slab.

Over the Kameniy bridge, traffic lights allow us to cross the roaring highways, back to our quiet area. Back through the park, again we see the disabled young man with his feet placed precariously on his footplates, a paper cup for handouts. He does not seem to attract passers-by.

We decide to pick up some supplies from a small upmarket food shop to try out for our forthcoming week long train ride. At the cash desk, Peter discovers that his cash is mainly Polish zlotys. The woman at the till very sweetly works out what we can afford to buy with our few roubles. Those zlotys, no one wants them. Pounds, euros, dollars, yes. Zlotys no. We get lost.

A woman stops to ask us what we are looking for. She says come with me, shows us where to safely cross the road, crosses the road with us, looks carefully at our map. Checks her iPhone and cheerfully wishes us well. For all Moscow's legendary rudeness it is far from the most unfriendly place we have been to.

Moscow Friday

On walking out of the hotel a breeze blows cool between the sun that warms us. The roadway is closed by barriers, leaving narrow strips either side for pedestrians. Soldiers with walkie-talkies. Then a few men walk past on the opposite pavement, then groups of men, then some obviously Muslim, bearded, with long flowing robes. They are being herded through security scanners, down a narrow alley to a mosque out of sight. This must be Friday prayers, Russian style. Beyond, a very opulent church. Inside women in head-scarves cross themselves and bow towards walls covered in paintings, golden frames glistening to the ceiling. They light candles, the light dancing on the floor. Above a painting of a black figure. It is striking, particularly as I have seen only one black person in the streets. We set off on the river bank heading west towards Gorky Park. It is an old industrial area, with names such as Manual Packing Area and the Red October Chocolate Factory. It looks like lower east side Manhattan, red brick warehouses with iron fire escapes. It has become a trendy place to hang out, lots of cafes, menus only in English and tiny boutiques. Towering above us is the absurd Peter the Great sculpture. It is at the end of a spit of land.

We realise we are on an island and are now heading back on ourselves. So we cross a bridge to the mainland, have another road to cross. The wheelchair hits a rut, two pedestrians rush up and grab the sides of the chair. An old woman walking with a crutch offers her assistance.

We are now on the south bank, pass under a huge highway and ahead is Gorky Park: an oligarch had spent millions renovating it We often see the Russian word for renovation, 'remont'. It serves to block access to many places.

Stop at the Caffe del Parco for a drink and to work on my blog. Outside the open window a man is hailing the public to come and sample the varieties of Italian ice cream. He has a striking angular face, hooked nose, dark hair. Not Russian looking. Every so often my train of thought is broken by his loud-hailer. Dream time. Cafe time.

Another of Stalin's wedding cakes, clearly a sister of the one we saw in Warsaw.

This monumental building style is another marker of areas within the former Soviet Union, along with the vast urban road schemes fenced from pedestrians, to allow rapid movement of the elite.

Pedestrians can only cross by deep subways, descending and re-ascending steep stairs.

Which means in the case of wheelchair users, not crossing roads at all.

We had previously encountered these in the Baltic states.

Here in Moscow we are confined to our urban island. The metro system seems to be totally inaccessible for us.

On past a long, many-waved roof sheltering booth after booth, each with a display of paintings for sale. Some have their makers sitting in deck chairs or at work with their brushes. The subjects ranging through bears in forests, imagined landscapes (perhaps owing something to Disney) to socialist realist idylls of happy peasants and youth league outings.

There is a small boy driving an electric car, his look of absolute elation as he reaches his mother sitting on a park bench.

The river is crossed with a monumental stone bridge, that passes high above us. It perhaps once carried a railway, but now has a continuous tent of glass running its length and is reserved for pedestrians.

We strike inland, following its course till it meets the ground where we can enter, along an open fretwork tube. We cross the river hoping there will be a way out for us at the other end.

The bridge finishes in a steep descent down escalators. No way. Then we notice a lift plastered with notices in Russian. There is a bell. We push it. Nothing. There is a voice on the intercom, unintelligible. Security? Perhaps warning us off. That time in no man's land.

A young security guard appears gesturing over his shoulder that he had to walk a long way from his office. He has a key which allows him to operate the lift. Smiles all round. We are again touched by someone trying to reach out to us and wish we could offer more in return.

Moscow is now often thought of as a city of roaring ten lane motorways and monstrous high rises. They of course exist and severely constrain our wanderings. But here are areas of nineteenth century three and four storey houses and very well to do. We came across the house Turgenev lived in the last years of his life, grand though made of wood, now decaying. Nearby a chauffeur eats sandwiches in his employer's Bentley

Time has passed and we need to head for home. We walk by the Moscow river with the lowering sun still providing warmth, the water glinting, a woman still drumming up custom through her megaphone for the next boat trip; an earlier boat could be seen chugging down the river with the Russian flag fluttering at the back. We reach the massive rebuilt Cathedral of Christ the Saviour – it had been blown up by order of Stalin, became a swimming hollow for years and then rebuilt 30 years ago. The map shows a pedestrian bridge extending from here right across the island to the south bank. We cross it, but the other side finishes in many steep stairs, so we retrace our steps looking for somewhere else to cross.

View of the recently rebuilt Cathedral of Christ the Saviour (extreme right of the picture), blown up on Stalin's orders in 1931. The site was then used as a public swimming pond for many years.
A lot of money has been spent on rebuilding and renewing churches since the collapse of communism.

We are hemmed in by uncrossable roads and vast buildings, but this area up to the river is very pleasant to wander around.

31

Retreat back to the Cathedral and follow the roads round to the heavily trafficked road bridge. (Is trafficking bridges an offence?).

Fortunately traffic lights with phases for pedestrians appear wherever we need them.

No evening in Moscow is complete without us getting lost trying to find our hotel, a woman gave us directions and sent us away with 'Enjoy your stay'.

I was surprised to see St George and his dragon, always thought as so English, (Cry 'God for Harry, England, and Saint George!') as the emblems of Moscow.

e **Moscow Times**

SINCE 1992

WWW.THEMOSCOWTIMES.COM

AUGUST 14 – 16, 2015   WEEKEND

Scandal Highlights Plight of Disabled

By Ilaria Parogni
newsreporter@imedia.ru

A high-profile incident in which Russian supermodel Natalia Vodianova's sister, who has autism and cerebral palsy, was made to leave a cafe for "scaring off clients" has elicited a storm of outrage on social networks, but disabled people and specialists say the incident is far from isolated and only illustrates the challenges faced by disabled people across the country.

"In our country, disabled people are regularly not allowed into expensive establishments or on planes, and are refused all sorts of services," Yevgenia Voskoboinikova, a Russian journalist and wheelchair user, told The Moscow Times. "If it wasn't for Oksana [Vodianova] being the relative of a model known everywhere around the world, no one would have known of the incident."

The episode that made headlines this week took place at a cafe in the sisters' native city of Nizhny Novgorod. Oksana Vodianova, 27, and her carer were asked to leave the premises of the Flamingo cafe for "scaring off their clients," the supermodel recounted in a Facebook post published Wednesday and widely shared on social media.

"Go get treatment, and get your kid treated too — and only then show up in a public place," the owner of the cafe told the carer, according to Vodianova's post.

The model noted that the cafe was virtually empty, and that the only other customer had told the owner to leave the two women alone. The owner threatened to call security, and Vodianova's mother, Larisa Kusakina, arrived at the establishment. After complaining to the owner about the treatment received by her daughter, she was detained by the police for disorderly conduct, according to Vodianova's post.

"When they took my mother to the local [police] station, they recognized her and were surprised; they said that they would not deal with the matter and that she should be taken to the central [police] station," Vodianova wrote. Kusakina

See DISABLED, Page 2

Moscow Saturday

Breakfast in our room on yoghurt and bananas. Tomorrow temperatures for Moscow are forecast to halve. The Moscow Times suggests everyone should enjoy the last of the summer concerts before winter sets in. We had imagined the whole of August as unbearably hot and had originally planned to come as late in the month as our visas allowed, so it's a good time to leave.

Around the corner is a man lying on the pavement, arms outstretched, shoeless. We cannot tell if he is drunk or ill. He looks drunk, unshaven. His eyes are closed. We carry on thinking of accounts that people here do not help, not because they do not care, but because they become wholly responsible for the casualty, even getting blamed for being the cause.

Ann suggested we eat lunch at the cafe near the Tretyakov gallery. That old adage of when not looking for something it can be easily found; the reverse seems true.

We pass the police station. Outside mugshots, criminals from central casting: bloated faces, bruises, cut lips, eyes already starting an argument.

Further on a black police cruiser stopped in the middle of the pavement. That fear evoked by the air of brutal power: are they wanting for some unknown reason to question us?

We had been advised to always carry passports as they are frequently checked, but they have not been so far and we are not carrying them. Drawing level with the cab we see the officer looking down, intent only on re-wrapping a bandage round his wrist.

Lost again we backtrack and see an ambulance has been called. Good.

Later we see the ambulance is still parked on the other side of the street, the man is still on the floor, while a road sweeper is determinedly sweeping around him, focused on his task. Life goes on.

Another Moscow strangeness: a side street blocked to traffic arranged with white benches and tables and bookshelves with some paperbacks. A reading street. More consumption of sandwiches than books. Intriguing.

Continuing east on the island we come out on the Ustinsky bridge. We have come too far. We ask directions to the gallery. People take our map and give directions we half understand. We wander back and forth, give up, then, giving up giving up, we find the gallery and gobble down a quick meal.

We have fifteen minutes before we should be back at the hotel, so we run past the old woman carrying the plastic cups of McDonald's coffee, the men from the Caucasus drilling in the street the vibrations passing through them like lightning and other men from the Caucasus washing the street with their orange hose and the painter up his ladder with his paintbrush poised in his hand for another stroke. Past the wedding parties, bride and groom looking serious followed by the photographer asking them to turn this way and that, followed by their light hearted friends.

Past the young women model, hip bones prominent, being asked to pose against a white wall, her pose emphasising her stick like figure.

The road is blocked with cars parked at odd angles. A biker has come off his motorbike, parts of which are lying strewn across the road, police in dark shirts with night sticks hung at their sides, other actors standing tensely waiting.

Returning to the hotel I do my stretches. We have paid a half day's stay to extend departure time to 6pm, but that is soon up, so downstairs to the dining area where we skulk awhile till the taxi comes.

Four and a half hours before boarding. Anxiety as to what awaits. Will we be able to get in the compartment?

The driver is a small dark haired man. He grips the wheel and drives furiously, racing the other vehicles along the huge highways.

The station looms like a castle, an old fantasy of Russia's frontier, the wild east rather than the Wild West.

We find the information kiosk and ask the woman behind the counter if she speaks any English she shakes her head.

'Beijing' This she hears as 'Berlin'.

We pause uncertain, then show our tickets. 'Ah, Pekin'. She passes a note through the hatch and waves her hand at it.

We must return at the time specified.

Distance (Km)	Hours ahead of Moscow	Train number & name: Days of running: Notes:	20 Vostok Every Saturday See note D
0	0	**Moscow** Yaroslavski station	23:45 Sat
461	0	Nizhni Novgorod	05:48 Sun
-	0	**St Petersburg** Ladozhki station	I
1,397	+2	Perm 2	20:17 Sun
1,778	+2	Yekaterinburg (Sverdlovsk)	01:59 Mon
2,676	+3	Omsk	13:53 Mon
3,303	+3	Novosibirsk	21:23 Mon
4,065	+4	Krasnoyarsk	09:07 Tue
5,152	+5	**Irkutsk** arrive	02:28 Wed
5,152	+5	**Irkutsk** depart	02:53 Wed
5,608	+5	Ulan Ude	11:22 Wed
5,864	+5	Naushki (Russian border) arrive	I
5,864	+5	Naushki (Russian border) depart	I
5,887	+5/+6	Suhe Bator (Mongolian border)	I
6,265	+5/+6	**Ulan Bator** arrive	I
6,265	+5/+6	**Ulan Bator** depart	I
6,770	+5/+6	Dzamin Uud (Mongolian border)	I
6,780	+5	Erlian (Chinese border) arrive	I
6,780	+5	Erlian (Chinese border) depart	I
6,626	+5	Zabaikalsk (Russian border) arr.	08:48 Thur
6,638	+5	Manzhouli (Chinese border) dep.	00:34 Fri
7,574	+5	Harbin (local time)	12:51 Fri
7,622**	+5	**Beijing** main station	05:46 Sat
8,492	+7	Khabarovsk	
9,258	+7	**Vladivostok**	

** Moscow-Beijing is 8,986 km (5,623 miles) via Harbin.

Four hours before departure.
We sit in the Business waiting room.

Full length swags curtain the ceiling-high windows, the floor is marble and, in the centre, among the huge overstuffed chairs, a full size shepherd and his lass forever chase each other round a windmill.

Quiet, emphasised somehow by the relentless violence of the television in the far corner.

At 11pm we are collected and ushered outside into a chill night, the dark tinged with maroon, made darker by the coloured lights of the shops and the houses with curtain-less windows. The platforms are some way distant from the station building.

Figures loom out of the dark to question our guide, but she shakes them off.

We start down our platform, past carriage after carriage. Eventually we stop and are helped on, into the compartment where we will spend the next eight days and seven nights, on the longest railway journey in the world.

What relief; the compartment is just for us and there is room for the wheelchair.

The route across the vastness of Russia

Sunday: day two on the trans-Sib

That feeling that you are finally doing what you have spent years talking about and imagining and then months planning is a strange mixture of great exhilaration, happiness but an odd sense of flatness, like the politician who wins the election and then wonders.

43

Our new home has two bunks, mine on the bottom has a white bar above which I can hold on to pull myself up. At either end of the bed are spot lights.

We discover my bed has three sections where it can fold through 30 degrees to raise the head or legs separately, like the electronic beds in the hospice. My back is resting on one of the joins, so we pad the bed out with blankets.

As there are only two of us in this compartment there is no need to fold the wheelchair up. It remains in the centre of the room. I am so pleased to see that the compartment is right next to the disabled toilet. I had fears of needing to walk for long distances between swaying carriages desperately trying to hold on.

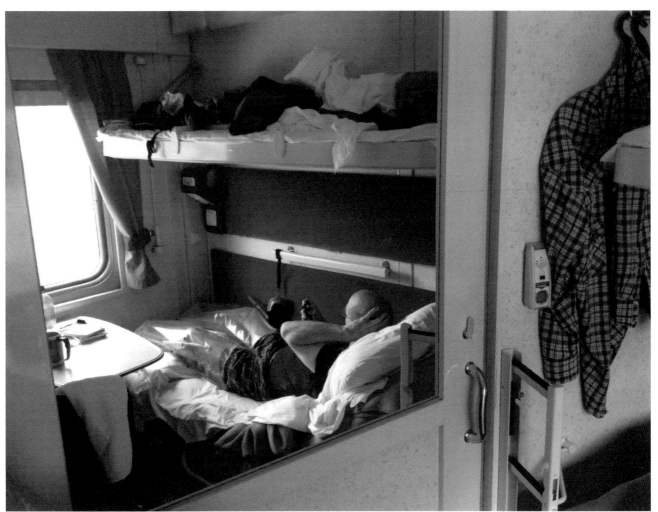

There is a grey box on the wall opposite my bunk. It is a digital display of the time in Moscow and temperature which remains at a constant 21 degrees, and alongside a red light indicating whether the toilet is occupied or not. On top are two red buttons to get a voice to intone the temperature and time. Above the box is a flat TV screen, which we half-heartedly try without success. It is useful for hanging clothes on. A rail which could be used for holding onto or walking along with the support of another person has instead become a place to hang towels. We have truly made ourselves at home here.

We are travelling through a landscape of birch trees mixed in with pine forests.

Farms flash by, brown outbuildings and tractors, occasionally the white of a satellite dish. I am surprised by this. I guess I should not be. How else would people get any reception here?

Siberia is a vast store of raw materials and energy that power our technological world.

A tall wiry looking man looks in through our open door. He is around 40, wearing glasses with a serious expression and a camera ready to hand. He is from Augsburg, travelling to Ulan Bator to meet his girlfriend who is flying there.

I venture into the toilet to test it out. It has a rail along one side which is reassuring as the train can suddenly lurch sharply as a counterpoint its normal swaying. There is a grab rail that can be brought down on the left of the WC to provide support. I had not noticed it before. I have good upper body strength so am able to hold myself up generally but am thrown against the rail with a sudden lurch. I just manage to regain balance.

My manual dexterity is poor so I find it hard to use my hands to make small movements like locking a toilet door. The older woman conductor did not understand this and said to Peter who was standing outside that he has to lock the door. Locking the door signals by red lights that the toilet is unavailable, saving people a trek up the corridor. I have now managed with practice to lock the door.

I find flushing the toilet completely impossible as it is operated by pressing down on a foot pedal. My feet do not do that.

We had an old guidebook, listing the route and times at station halts. However we find it puzzling as it uses Moscow times and it lists stations that the train no longer stops at. The train moves through six time zones which makes it difficult to keep a grasp on what day and what time it is at any point. Every so often we stop at a station. I can't see their names.

The only people we have so far seen in the endless countryside.

The platforms are low, the steps narrow and near vertical and there is a big gap at the bottom; there is no way I can get off or on the train when it halts.

49

We eat food that Peter buys, pot noodles, with hot water from the carriage's samovar. I am still trying to learn how to curl noodles on to my fork in preparation for the real task ahead, eating noodles in China. Munching our way through crisps, bananas, the other finds from Peter's foraging expeditions at stations, is not the most balanced of diets but when you are travelling I long ago learned that you eat when and what you can.

The sky darkens from blue to a thunderous grey. The next moment night has enveloped us. Taking this as a signal I went to bed. Peter using the narrow footholds at the side settles himself down on the top bunk at the end of a momentous day.

Monday: day three on the trans-Sib

I woke this morning stiff and aching. I had been scared to turn over as I could not work out how to do it. I would have had to hold on to the bar against the wall above as I rolled my knees away from the bed. But the table was in the way, there was nothing to stop me rolling onto the floor.

Better lie here in this constrained curl.

I do not want to miss anything. The view does not change, then it is different, the ordinary becomes extraordinary, each change to be savoured.

A woman's purple umbrella signifying the next station.

We ate from our provisions, salami and cheese and tea. A mug of hot water from the samovar with a tea bag and a heaped spoon of milk powder the consistency of grated cheese.

Pass a dilapidated brown bridge, falling back into the land like most of the buildings outside the cities.

There is a young Chinese woman travelling on her own to Beijing and then onwards to her home in Hong Kong.

Asked by the German man what she was doing she replied 'just travelling'.

The black-haired conductor vacuumed the carpet in the corridor while our door was open and then came in and did the strip in our compartment.

The older blond woman with the floral bib got a damp cloth to wipe dirt from the vinyl area.

The Samovar, grand and romantic title, but rather a disappointment. And the water is never boiling.

Peter's foraging trips bring back all manner of food that I hope is edible, a cake with sausage cooked in it, very solid brown bread.

Tuesday: day four on the trans-Sib

It is very hot in our compartment, the air is still and the heat cloying.

I cannot sleep. Every so often I turn my head to look at the digital clock: 02:22 and then what seems like many hours later 02:23, alternately mesmerised and frustrated by a clock that doesn't move.

The kvass Peter bought earlier tastes like the dandelion and burdock we drank in Cologne.

We tethered the kvass and the milk to a leg of the table as the swaying jolting rock and roll of the train set them spinning.

We had just discovered this strap that was probably designed to secure a wheelchair to the wall.

We continue to make these small discoveries in hidden corners.

Peter slept badly too. It isn't very comfortable up there as his bed has sharp bits sticking in him.

Endless birch trees stretch to the horizon

We get up and eat some instant porridge which, because the water is off the boil, turns out as a thin gruel. I am hungry and it is eaten. We share out the food and then feeling tired relieved to put our heads on the pillows hoping to be soon drifting off to sleep.
The birch and pine landscape still dominates. Seemingly endless trains of oil tankers pass. I notice a purple flower growing in great clumps on the hillside.
Now we are passing sandy, boggy land.

We reach another station. Peter uses the opportunity to dash out of the train, take photos and to stock up on what supplies he can scavenge; always fearful of the train departing without him.
He returns with crisps and a bottle of pickled gherkins, a great Russian speciality, if 'Beginners Teach Yourself Russian' is to be believed. I have been missing my morning cup of coffee so he also brings back a tin of Nescafe and a plastic bottle of milk.

The scrum to buy food at a station kiosk. How long before the train leaves?

The landscape unrolls endlessly

Wednesday: day five on the trans-Sib

Having had a much better sleep, although Peter complains to have slept only fitfully again, we get up, excited to see Irkutsk. In our original plans we were to stay here for several days before journeying the 50 odd kilometres to Lake Baikal. We planned to take a ferry across the lower part of the lake before journeying down to rejoin the train at Ulan Ude. Unfortunately the Baikal ferry stops running early August, hunkering down for the start of the long winter. That information changed our minds. We can carry enough clothes in our one rucksack for one season only. A HOT one.

Clocks keep Moscow time; 2.45 am. Afternoon in Irkutsk.

Irkutsk station

Shared taxi outside the station heading for
Ulan-Ude

Irkutsk.

Everyone knew to stock up with food for the days ahead. Peter, unfortunately, didn't. He just took pictures, whilst I of course was stuck on the train.

The train goes alongside Lake Baikal for about two hours, a delicious combination of an azure cloudless sky and a shimmering turquoise expanse of water.

For the most part the landscape has been hacked at, imposed upon, an endless relentless opponent, rather than appreciated for its splendour.

Huge factories and extraction industries and accompanying settlements built without thought for the environment.

Here by Baikal there is by contrast a holiday industry in the stunning scenery, though through it always the endless trains of oil, wood, crushed stone, coal. Slowly moving across this vast landscape makes us realise how small and insignificant we actually are, how little time we would last here without our technological carapace. Winter here is more brutal than anywhere on earth. Through great tracts of land there are no signs of human activity.

A Russian family get on at the next station, a whirl of arms and legs. Russians clearly enjoy being with their children. We hear them singing in the next carriage. They play games with the young Chinese woman. They behave so easily with others, friendly and not demanding. We pass through an area that is stark by its very loss, Earth has been eaten away in the name of strip mining. As the sun sets lower and lower amongst the trees, a glowing halo of energy, the earth is bathed in a soft brown light.

I have an early night as I am suffering from spasms. Imagine if you can a terrible cramp coupled with a sense that you are being pinned down by invisible hands, able to take fewer and fewer breaths and then you have an idea how it feels. I often have to just wait until the pain subsides.

Changing position and sleep can help. The pain makes me very tired, I try to read a little but cannot concentrate. The text is jumping up and down so I drop the Kindle. Sleep rapidly takes me over.

Once off the train you then have to be able to leave the station. This is not one for us. Hopefully things will improve.

Thursday: day six on the trans-Sib

We are awoken in the middle of the night by an unlocking of our door. The woman with the dark hair is standing there with a man who had, unasked, stored a huge box on the ledge above. In that moment when you are between the worlds of sleep and full awareness, Peter lets out a strangled yelp, the man enters, lifts the box down and they back out of the door. the woman saying sorry, sorry.

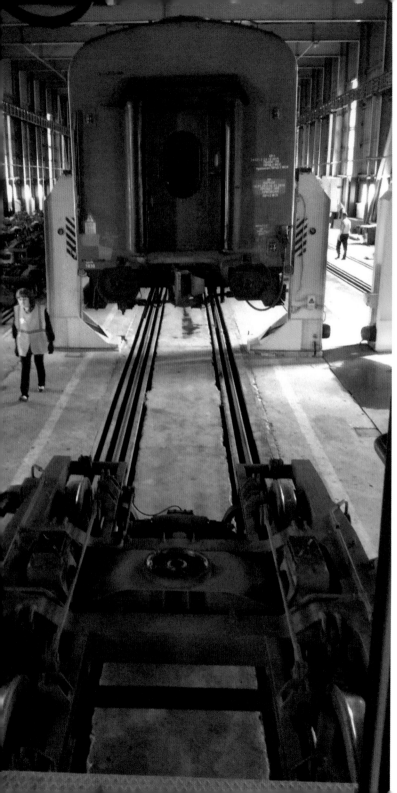

We are at a station and the man departs with his package.

Peter gets up and hunts for food in the dark, but there is no kiosk here. Last night's dinner was crisps, stale bread and miso soup from a packet we have been carrying for months.
I haven't felt deprived or hungry. I came to explore, for the experience, not to eat. In that context food takes on a different quality.

The train is shunted into a goods yard, the first of many thundering stops, finally coming to rest with much shaking and slamming of brakes in a vast hangar.
Here we stayed as the workmen decoupled the carriages and one by one unbolted the wheel assembly, jacked the carriage up and slid in the replacement set of wheels.
Through this the Russian crew slept.

We are shunted back to the station, the other passengers board and the Russian immigration officials arrive, asking for our passports.

She looked at the five year old photograph that I had used for my visa, asked me to take off my glasses, knelt down and looked at me lying down, then called her colleague to look. I had a rising sense of panic. Never use an old photograph in an official document to save the bother of having a new one taken!

Her colleague instructed me sternly, don't smile. I wasn't smiling, I was feeling mildly sick.

After much discussion and several visits to peer at me (lying on my bed writing this), they seemed to be convinced it was me.

Then followed the customs official who after asking how many roubles we had on us, opened an unnoticed panel in the ceiling, looked around with his torch and departed. Peter went into the corridor to photograph an extraordinary glowing sunset when the Chinese border officials came in. A tall thickset man, "No photographs". He hands us our entry and exit cards which asks us for 'our address in China'. We are in China!

It is 19:44. Manzhouli Station.

The Cyrillic train indicator boards which we could puzzle out have vanished; all is now in Chinese characters which leave us utterly illiterate.

A torch flashes underneath the train. Checking for contraband or migrants?

On the opposite platform the carriages have ramps that the conductors fit. But our carriage doors are, for the first time since Moscow, almost level with the platform.

Another young official comes into the carriage with a portable probe, checks our temperatures from two feet away and then turning to Peter asks "What's wrong with him?"

"He has cerebral palsy and cannot walk."

"I'm sorry" he says and leaves. Another official opens the door and rapidly closes it when we ask if he wants to see our passports. A customs official with white gloves asks where is my luggage. We are clearly under-luggaged.

He thinks he has found something when he extracts a wrapped package from the high shelf: drawing paper.

Peter shows him a drawing of me he was making while the immigration official was doubting my identity. "Very good", he says and leaves.
We spot an immigration official walking past the compartment.
We give her the completed entry papers and passports, she gives a start and looks visibly shocked. Sighing she reaches for her walkie talkie and speaks to her colleague.

We can tell from the rising tone of her voice that a serious mistake has been made, clearly somebody was supposed to come, check our documents and then take them away to be scanned we guess.

Later the official is joined by a more senior male colleague. She makes an unmistakable sweeping motion with her hand as if to say 'We walked right past this compartment and were sloppy'.

Suddenly a burst of activity, the immigration officials demand that the Russian crew open up all the hidden spaces as they will need to be checked.

Having it seemed to have satisfied themselves that there were no people hidden away in the cracks and crevices of the train, another young customs official returns with our documents,

"All fine, no problems" he says smiling as he hands them back. We head for bed still in a state of shock that we are actually in China!

We cross several very broad rivers

The countryside is looking more cared for somehow.

Friday: day seven on the trans-Sib

A cacophony of noise stirs my sound sleep.
This loud unfamiliarity drags me awake, resolving into a repeated clearing of throat and spitting. A workman with smokers' catarrh? I wait in the corridor outside the toilet. Everyone is using ours. It's so much bigger than the others at each end of the carriages.

He is spending a long time in there, clearing his tubes.

Eventually the door slides open and a petite woman emerges. How did she make so much noise?

A Chinese man approaches us: Russian? he says hopefully and starts speaking in Russian to us. Clearly he wants to have a chat. He looks disappointed at our response. Not for the first time on this trip we are not able to offer more.

Outside, marshland, visible pools of standing water giving way to chimney stacks and crowds of nodding donkeys, though not visibly nodding, scattered everywhere, extracting oil by the bucket load. The Russian crew have all but given up. The lead conductor has shed her uniform. This new lax attitude is shown by the toilets remaining unlocked during station stops. They were locked before as the WC empties straight onto the track. This locking was rather inconvenient when we had to stay twelve straight hours on the train while crossing the border, but the old-fashioned WC has two great advantages; it doesn't smell and it doesn't block when 'foreigners' throw toilet paper down it. (We, as obvious non-locals, had been accused of blocking the toilet on the train to Moscow and our disavowal had been disbelieved. One of the few times we were made to feel unwelcome.)

Harbin in the rain. Among the modernity remain corrugated roofs covering low dwellings with yards or gardens.

We stop here for twenty minutes but there is nothing to buy on the platform. The guide book had described the many foods available, but all the stations we see are free of vendors or even kiosks.

I am grateful for the miso soup that I brought with me from the UK and the solid brown, although still tasty, loaf, that Peter bought in Irkutsk.

Changchun station, an anonymous tent like structure full of glass and underground lighting. Peter is not allowed on to the platform. He comes back to report to me that the station has level access. We may be able to use these stations. We shall see. Across the tracks we see a woman in a wheelchair being pushed towards a lift. In both Changchun and Siping we see rows upon countless rows of large scale tower blocks, it becomes difficult to tell where the city stops and the suburbs begin. These cities themselves like the station feel characterless.

Saturday: day eight on the trans-Sib.

A lovely sight for a wheelchair user. I am now able to get off the train.
Well I would be able to if I were able to manoeuvre more quickly, but Peter has taken this encouraging picture for me.

Beijing day one

I awake several times in the night looking up at the digital clock and working out how many hours, how many minutes it is before I have to get up, working forward from Moscow time. The train is scheduled to arrive into Beijing at 05:46 am local time.

Peter's time frazzled brain had set the alarm on the iPad for 13:00.

Suddenly the main train lights are switched on, the Russian crew prepare for their next set of new arrivals. In eight days I did not get off the train nor go to the dining car. That was three carriages away with unpassable connections between them - wide spaces with no hand holds, in unpredictable motion. Think rapids, tidal whirlpools. Peter did once make the trip and found only tiny packets of peanuts at vast expense.

I spent most of the time in the compartment. We sometimes left the door open, but the train's uncertain movement would slam it shut.

I rarely saw other passengers. By now they are all Chinese and talking is difficult. So you need to be able to get along with your companion. Peter and I have travelled together for three decades. We sat in the carriage, looked out of the window, listened to my MP3 player, chatted, told stories, cracked jokes and watched the world wander gently by.

Beijing station. The platform was level with the carriage, so straight off, down a ramp ribbed, not smooth, but no steps and we are out. Easy! If the Trans Siberian journey is relatively peaceful, Beijing at 5:45 a.m. is not, people rushing to and fro, going everywhere.

Peter could not hear me when I tried to speak. People fill the scene, the volume on max, our ears and eyes now had to adjust after only two hours sleep, bleary eyed and somewhat delirious. Now what?

There are people, parked cars, then railings, several sets bounding the highway; the only way to cross is by bridge, up two steep flights of stairs. We watched as the crowds ascended and descended. No way for us. "Taxi?" Someone points. A group of old men. We showed them the piece of paper with details of the hotel, they crowded around for a closer look. We start negotiating. They want 100 yuan. Offer 60, it is only over there, pointing. Two drivers offer 80. Ok, we are tired, tourists are there to be overcharged.

The driver roughly grabbed my arms, opened the door pushed my body inside and tried forcing my legs in after as Peter struggled to disassemble and fold the wheelchair.

I collapse backwards on to the seat. As he slammed the door I was struggling to pull myself upright. Peter is in front buried under luggage. I hoped we had managed to load all the parts of my chair.

The driver drives fast down big roads, big buildings, then turning away from the chaos, a very narrow lane, a different city. He asks for our piece of paper again, with directions in Chinese, looks dubious. His uncertainty passes to us, but suddenly there it is, our courtyard hotel. After the mega city, a rural feel; bamboo and a mynah bird greeting us "nie hao", Good Morning.

Three shallow steps through the front door.

It's not yet 6:30 am.

Check in is six hours away but the young quietly smiling receptionist welcomes us, directs us to the bar area, a low ceilinged dark place with Wi-Fi; eight days without shows our reliance, but soon quenched.

We are then offered buffet breakfast, dumplings and fruit.

First footsteps in our new land, released from the confines of our rocking boat.

A mix of the exotic; Arabic lettering announce a Muslim restaurant

We want to explore, so out into the early morning heat, a benign warmth that welcomes us like an old friend. Light, air, movement, we walk down our quiet lane, the quiet unbroken by the frequent electric scooters, motorbikes, 3-wheeled delivery vehicles weaving among the pedestrians. They assume the right of way until challenged by something bigger.

87

We walk on, past the barber's shop with the dog lolling outside, the children sitting in plastic chairs outside their parents' flower shop stretching and yawning in the heat, past the young women holding their umbrellas against the sun, dodging a middle-aged woman on a bicycle with a visor covering her face.

Back at the hotel, the room is ready hours before check-in. I can't get into the bathroom. They move a chest of drawers out of our way, with the comment that the feng shui is better that way; the wheelchair can now get to the door. After 8 days I am ready for a shower, but how? I suggest folding the wheelchair so, reversed, I can hold the handles like a walking frame and squeeze past.

The room phone wakes us from our afternoon snooze.

We are invited to dinner, friends of a Chinese friend in London. M, a commercial lawyer and his wife and son, who is on the point of moving to the U.S. to study.

The restaurant they take us to is enormous. It is so large that it crosses an alleyway and spreads into a warren of buildings beyond. Outside on the main road crowds besiege the manager for tickets to queue. We go straight in, leaving staff to park our Audi SUV. We thread the alleys, the various buildings, winding past a tank bluely lighting a large fish unaware of nearby cooks chopping their bretheren.

A pomegranate tree loaded with fruit shelters our table. We are sat spaced around a large round table. A turntable at the centre is successively loaded with dishes and at a signal from the host we start eating.

I do not have the manual dexterity to use chopsticks so need a fork. Despite the smartness of the restaurant they don't have one. I was offered a spoon.

Fantastic food, especially after a week on crisps and thin porridge.

Stuffed, we retrace our path to the front where the largest room is. Here they are putting on a show: juggling a watering can with hugely extended spout, occasionally pausing to pour a fine stream of water from a great height into a tiny pot. Then a man comes on moulding and blowing slabs of pastry into balloons. The show ends with a dancer from the opera, changing colours and characters with a quick succession of masks.

A commemoration of the victory over Japan in the Second World War has been suddenly announced and the whole of the Forbidden City is closed off by army and police. Our hosts want to show us Tienanmen Square.

We drive fruitlessly in wide circles but can't approach it.

They drop us where our little alley branches from the main road.

As we walk towards the hotel, the owners of the hardware store recognise us, wave and say hello.

I smile. I think we are going to like Beijing.

Beijing day two

It is extraordinary the contrasts, the vegetable sellers and the hairdressers drying their towels, the hutong and the big roaring city beyond, hoping every detail that catches our eye will help the attempt to understand the whole, that city of 20 million people that attracts many millions more as economic migrants from all over China.

Peter finds a doorway that interests him. He is interested in the square patterns that recur everywhere at all levels, from small patterns in fabric to the layout of this city itself.

I am amazed by the smoothness of pavements. In London an uneven paving stone can tip my chair forward. Then you might see my legs can have a mind of their own, they shoot forward off the foot rests and pain shoots through me. I haven't yet experienced that here.

There are pedestrian bridges over roads, but they have steps and sometimes ramps, but steep and anyway too narrow for the wheelchair. We can only cross where there are traffic lights. So we wait and wait. This gives me an opportunity to look at the people around me, a grandmother on the back of a three-wheeler, the lovers on a bike, she riding side saddle and the little boy being carried in state in a three-wheeler. Blue shirted volunteers with red armbands, (known as Capital Security Volunteers) are dotted around the city, mainly it seems elderly retired people sitting in booths, on the ground, or on deckchairs.

Some grunt at you and simply point and others talk, regardless of the fact that we cannot understand them. We had been warned that people were unfriendly and distant. We have found the opposite.

The wind signals a sudden change in the weather, picking up leaves, throwing grit and sand, darkening the sky. It looks like a storm is about to hit. We look for shelter through eyes half closed against the dust and head for a mall.

Inside we decided weathering the weather is better than this so familiar consumer trash and go back out. Pushing on against the wind, we find ourselves in a Russian district. It was comforting to be able to read the Cyrillic script, once so foreign. At least we had a key to it. Chinese characters are beautiful but are an unknown ocean. The Russian area had clearly once had grandeur, perhaps in early Sino-Soviet days. That time had passed. Everything was run down.

We wander into a huge Russian market building, a maze of alleys between stalls piled with every kind of ugly consumer good: hats, watches, sunglasses, tennis rackets, mobiles, clothing, nameless things from a nightmare.

Stall holders barter and cajole in a mixture of Russian, Chinese and English.

We buy a device to enable us to download images from my camera to the iPad. Unsurprisingly when we get it back to the hotel we find it doesn't work.

Next time I buy anything, I will think of this market and know that the item probably spent part of its journey to me in a place like this.

Eventually we find Ritan Park, chosen at random from our map. The weather still glowered and we look for shelter. Passing a rock carved with calligraphy, we feel constantly like archaeologists trying to decipher the unknown and only just brushing the surface with our fingers.

We pass a toddler and his parents turn to him "Say hello", he looks away and they say hello, waving. I love the way people smile and wave at us when parting. Walking further we came across a group of women dressed all in pink, moving rhythmically to music.

Another group of couples are ballroom dancing, a bald man in a black shirt showing the steps.

We watch small groups of people playing cards under the watchful eye of a bronze sage.
Curious bystanders gather around, absorbed in the play.

Time was against us as we had a date with a duck. M. is taking us to a restaurant, "1949", that specialises in roast duck. I assume a political reference, perhaps, but the restaurant is housed in a building of that date. M picked us up in his Mercedes: the SUV has a number plate ending in an even number and today only odd numbered cars are allowed in Central Beijing. Hence two cars. We are very surprised to see in this expensive restaurant many men in shorts, as is our host. We had been advised that shorts were almost indecent. Have things changed?

Beijing day three

 At first new, bewildering but soon a routine takes over. To breakfast.

Our room is at the end of an inner courtyard - an open area with chairs shaded by trees, a covered walkway on all four sides - so across our courtyard, turn right across the end of the next, through two doors, past the delightful receptionists to the breakfast room.

My wheelchair as usual does not fit under the table. I have to sit sideways on, the path from plate to

mouth uncertain. Liquids particularly don't like the trip. A trial when travelling with only one change of clothes. There is a buffet of western and Chinese foods. The western foods, like the very few westerners we have seen, look foreign, unhealthy. We breakfast on dumplings, watermelon, fruits I can't name but can recall the taste, and fresh pineapple, at first avoided as all I knew was tinned, now longed for.

A mynah bird in a cage by the door every so often shrieks "ni hao", unnerving because of my startle reflex [7]

Whilst doing my exercise programme we watch CCTV news from Beijing in English; the irony of the acronym has not passed me by. The newscaster is an African American, presumably for American consumption as we haven't seen anyone with obvious African ancestry here. There is an emphasis on the upcoming commemoration of the war of resistance against the Japanese aggression, our Second World War. It fascinates me how a country chooses to present itself to the world.

Travelling, we have seen British, Russian, French, American, Italian and I think Taiwanese TV, for others' consumption.

Then through the hutong listening to the now familiar sounds: the clearing of throats and spitting; the ghostly hum of an electric bike; the bumping of a gas canister being pulled along; the honking of the driver bringing his cardboard boxes to the rubbish dump next to the soldier's post where they stand like male Barbie dolls, motionless; the police station, the men chattering before going out on shift.

Threading across the bigger streets we reach the outer walls of the Forbidden City and follow them to a moat separating Tienanmen (the main gate and square) from the inner gate leading into the Forbidden City. The whole area around Tienanmen is cordoned off for two weeks (presumably to avoid protests). The Forbidden City itself also is closed for the two weeks. This closure was announced suddenly a few days ago, and included the closure of hotels and museums in a wide area around the Forbidden City. Nightmare for tour operators, but great for us as there are almost no western tourists.

 We cross Chang'an, the huge road running east west through Tienanmen; only possible with police assistance. We were standing in front of the pedestrian underpass looking helpless, and they hold the traffic up for us to cross. Past the upturned bowl of the performing arts centre, across another vast road, with traffic lights - our wanderings are contained by uncrossable roads, those with bridges, not traffic lights.

This morning we have a goal, but the route to it is determined by chance and the uncrossable, like playing snakes and ladders.

Now small roads again. We take side streets and come across a strip of park, with men playing mahjong to attentive spectators. Then just before our first goal a terrible snake, a fenced road crossable only by bridge. Defeat. We pause for reflection and notice something extraordinary.

This bridge, uniquely, has a lift. And it works. And there is another lift at the other side! We take a photo. A police officer comes over, wondering what we are doing, realises our pleasure and smiles.

This first goal is a long street specialising in calligraphy, paper, brushes and finished scrolls. Peter has a long-standing interest in calligraphy so was as he said in 'minor heaven'.

We watched a man in his workshop writing. Like Chinese cooking, a lot of preparation before the calm but quick execution. There is a woman selling brushes. Peter tests brushes by painting on special paper that wetted show brush marks that soon fade away. They barter, she writing her price, he, his counter offer. Further along a man writing characters in water on the street with a brush the size of a kitchen mop. We are careful not to tread on his work.

Hunger hits, and there is a small cafe selling dumplings. The woman hands us a menu with the translation in English. We point and hold fingers to show the quantity. We watch the woman roll out the pastry and fill the dumplings before dropping them into a pan of boiling water. Now on the last leg of our exploration to find Ox street mosque. A man across the road spots our uncertainty and gives directions. We try to follow, but after a while stop, uncertain. He cycles up behind us to point the way again.

Ox Street mosque, more Chinese than Middle Eastern, a series of courtyards, then the prayer hall. Inside Peter took his shoes off and pulls me in my wheelchair over the steep door step. A very old man with long wizened beard comes over and says something, then points downwards. Peter starts to take off my shoes still he points. Presumably it's the wheels he dislikes touching the carpet. We roll out.

Under an arch an older man is sitting at a table with a crowd around him. He has a round face with a smile that could power a city, few teeth and a white Islamic cap.

He is painting cats, as people eagerly point out, in a single movement of the brush.

He uses his left hand to draw a male cat, the right, a female.

Is there symbolism in that?

He paints one of each for us.

When it is explained to him that we are from England, he holds up a photograph of himself meeting the lead of the musical Cats when it played here 15 years ago, the Chinese cat man meeting the English cat.

The explanation comes from three young women who are here as part of their philosophy degree.

I am not sure what they were learning but it was clearly fun.

Arabic calligraphy decorates this huge vase

A female cat

A male cat

We find a taxi. The driver is helpful and understands when we pronounce our destination. Minor triumph. The journey is along vast highways, unrecognisable as the city we had earlier walked. The meter fare seems so low we tip generousy. The driver is very happy.

Eat at a cafe. No translations or pictures. A young man helps us order.

He thinks I am Peter's younger brother. Unfamiliarity with western faces makes age recognition difficult. Noodles with meat sauce, delicious like all the food we've eaten here. We notice other customers asking the young man about us.

Workmen at a nearby table loudly slurping soup cheerily greet us as they leave.

Back to our lane, we buy our ritual yoghurt drink - sweet yoghurt in a pot drunk through a straw. The woman shop owner has a kind face and friendly greeting and knows our ritual. She punches the straws through the lids and hands them to us.

I feel I am beginning to understand, if not China then something of its people. I like what I am finding.

Beijing day four

In the Middle East jinns are feared, as we learn from Tahir Shah's 'In Arabian Nights'. Here the bad spirits are held at bay by the design of the courtyard houses and in particular by a wooden plank creating a threshold that has to be stepped over at the front door. We had been warned that we would have great difficulty getting the wheelchair into buildings because of them.
This is the first we have seen.

Cross the seething highway, step out of the motor world into a Hutong, but this is on the tourist route.

For the first time we are hassled, by rickshaw drivers.

The canal leads to an ornamental lake north of the Forbidden City.
There are three heads in the water, which is dark green. They are swimmers.
Next to us is a sign banning swimming (in English and Chinese). It is intriguing that in this society people are openly breaking the rules, and challenging our preconceptions of an always obedient people.
A swimmer emerges next to us, slim as most people are. It is just the children of the well-off that tend to fatness.

We come to a cafe, the first we have found.

People hang out on the street, in parks, on benches; they visit noodle places to slurp their food then leave,

but there doesn't seem to be a place they go to hang out and sip tea. We had kept hoping to find one, to sit, absorb, to people watch. This is a spot for tourists to pause in their punishing pursuit of sightseeing. We order a yoghurt drink.

A young Chinese girl is twirling a length of ribbon attached to a stick, absorbed in the changing colours.

We are swept up in the crowds, all Chinese, past the tacky, past a reggae themed bar, Bob Marley wailing.

We find a Western-style cafe with Wi-Fi and coffee. Inside I lose all sense of China and drift back to the Finchley Road.

As I work on my blog I glance around: a family sitting opposite taking photographs of their little daughter, an old man asleep, all jammed together. The coffee is good but costs nearly £4 a cup, more than we spent on lunch for two. Rich and poor.

We head for home, walking past the Capital Security Volunteers, here middle-aged women waving red flags to marshal the bus stop queue in rush hour.

In the evening when we head out to eat it is already pitch black. Lighting is subdued and the electric bikes unlit along the alley.

We find a very local restaurant. We can't see what they serve but it is very busy. Heave up the steps, through the door, the walls are grey cinder block. I am not certain who is a customer, who staff. Everyone sitting at long tables. A man who was serving sits down with his friends.

We order shrimp as an alternative to oyster which we now see is what everyone else is eating. They arrive, large and whole. We are novices at dismembering corpses but what we manage is sweet and tender. Major clean up required.

Heading for home we pass the yoghurt shop, the woman smiles at me, puts the straw in the pot and hands it up.

Thanks.

I find small movements like handling straws difficult.

I haven't been laughed at or patronised here.

We continue, the owners of the hardware shop say hello and wave.

I feel at home.

Beijing day five

Leisurely start. Ask reception about buses. They discourage.
Eventually find us route 701 from nearby major cross roads that goes
near the arty 798 area, the goal for today.

The bus stop is on a busy six lane highway.

Lots of buses come past, a few low-floor, others have steep steps.

701 comes, stops, gone too quickly for us to respond. After twenty
minutes or so another arrives.

We are ready, but entry is difficult. The door next to the driver is too
narrow for us. We have to use the middle door. The first step is
about two feet above the ground, then a further two shallow but
deep steps.

The driver is in a huge hurry. Peter struggles with the wheelchair.
The driver comes to help, grabs another passenger, they take the
front of the wheelchair, Peter the back. I am at 45 degrees. Peter
staggers, but manages to hold on as I am manhandled in.

There is a young woman conductor sat in a box to the left of the
door. Peter shows her the address written by the hotel and starts
paying the 3 yuan fare each. The bus accelerates rapidly and I am
thrown backwards, just saved from hitting my head by Peter and
another quick passenger.

The bus is quite crowded. The conductress evicts an elderly woman from her corner seat on the opposite
side of the door and Peter is made to sit there, anchoring the wheelchair, with a pole for me to grab on.

It's a long ride, and the driver is fierce, the ride a series of rough acceleration and braking to loud blasts on
the horn, leaning on its long lever to the right of his steering wheel.

I am bracing myself against the noise, then try to hide behind a wall of MP3 music.

Stops are infrequent and short.

Suddenly he yells at us to get off. The most short-tempered man we've met here. We are slow. But he
comes to help us off.

We wander the streets, massive commercial developments, business parks, shopping malls.

We eat in a fast food restaurant in one such block, a great meal, too much, but we devour it, dumplings with very spicy sauce, more food we had forgotten we had ordered.

Eventually we find the
798 area.
The whole grid of
streets here small scale,
trees, galleries;
Shoreditch cool.

A cage of red
dinosaurs, for some
reason.

A huge William Kentridge show, fantastic

Can't get a taxi, ring M: he will send a driver about 5pm, in an hour or so.

I need to stretch, having been sitting so long and remember the huge cushions with visitors sprawled on them in the arts centre, dim lights, pretentious video, ideal for a stretch. We go back in. As I lunge from the wheelchair onto a cushion in the enveloping gloom, the guard looks at us strangely but says nothing. M's wife and his secretary arrive in a 2 door Mercedes; this is their car for odd days with its odd numbered license plate. The Audi SUV is for even days.

Goodbye Beijing, Hello Xi'an

It was with a real sense of loss that we said goodbye to the Double Happiness hotel. No happiness without bitterness? Hotel staff normally measure out their politeness, and I can understand that, having to be nice to everyone must be a trial. But here we felt like guests. It was perhaps the first time I have enjoyed hanging round a hotel during the day.

The courtyard was attractive and peaceful.

Watching small children's fascination with the garden swings I remember as a small child my delights were with the immediate, not with whatever grand sites or sights parents thought important.

There are no western tourists left here. Is that because of the sudden closure of the Forbidden City? We couldn't have chosen a better time.

An employee of the hotel takes our belongings in a rickshaw to the end of the lane where M had promised to meet us.

He turns up late which makes for a tense journey through heavy traffic, veering between lanes, looking for advantage. Beijing West Station is immense, the approach roads strung like spaghetti flung at random round some 1920s view of the future.

First we must show tickets and IDs to get through the outer door then pass through security, then into the huge hall with its countless waiting rooms organised by train number. Show your tickets to enter. This is why they advise early arrival.

They are well organised for disabled passengers. There's a special area, with a woman in charge who organises our dispatch via lift (kept locked) to the platform level onto the very newest, smartest fastest train, the white painted, bullet nosed Gaotie train.

 It has the look and feel of an airplane. There is a conductor for every door. She, realising our reserved seats were some way down the carriage, asked the man sitting by the door to swap with us.

The train glided out of the station, little sensation of speed as the track is raised well above the surroundings and is very smooth, the only indication, a digital readout '312 kph'.

 I work on my blog while Peter talks to a young man who had recently driven to Tibet with his wife and proudly scrolled through the images on his smartphone, mostly of his wife posing in a landscape, some of monks (taken discretely as 'they didn't like to be photographed').

Seems so odd that you can drive to Tibet for a holiday. Too mundane.

Vast fields and huge cities flash past. One city enveloped in smog, which we have fortunately not yet encountered.

Every so often I look up as the countryside flashes by, a woman dressed like a cinema usherette selling ice cream, a grandmother opposite teaching her grandson to count as he lies spread eagled on her lap, then tenderly rubbing his hair as he slept. She reached over and helped me with a packet of tissues I was having trouble with.

Mountains appear on the horizon as we approach Xi'an.

Xi'an North station, another huge new development. Ramped underground exit, to the orderly queue for taxis. The new station is a long way from town and we hope that on the way in the driver might work out quite where our hotel is. He seemed very uncertain when handed the hotel booking which had the address in Chinese, which we can't read. Our map is in English only, which he can't read. Night is falling fast.

Traffic is horrendous and driving standards atrocious. Strange these people so courteous in person are pitiless behind a steering wheel. The only rule is size; bicycles scatter pedestrians, are themselves meat for taxis, which only stop for buses.

He keeps asking for the piece of paper, and now we are in the old city, a rectangle bounded by city walls and bisected by North-South, East-West roads, he finally stops to ask passers-by for directions. Eventually after an hour of driving that felt like five, he pointed upwards. Illuminated against the night sky "Citadines", a French apart type of hotel. It lacks character but is spacious, except of course the bathroom. I'd like a word with architects who design disabled bathrooms. Did they ever try to manoeuvre a wheelchair in one?

After stretching we set out to explore. We are separated from the Muslim quarter, which has the night market for food. There is the usual pedestrian subway, with lots of steps. So just walk along the road and hope. And this time hope is rewarded with traffic lights. Across the road, through a hole in the line of buildings we are suddenly in a different world, dominated by people, walking, carrying, eating, buying,

selling. Lights puncture the darkness. Food stalls, shops, fruit, nuts, cakes, sweets, walnuts, pomegranates, bunches of big black grapes, frying tofu, kebabs. The sticks used to spear the meat pile up discarded in bins, so many, like upside down Christmas trees. Noodle shops, barkers shouting each other down to attract business, dumplings. Here we go in one and eat, the delightful fire in our throats add to the noise, heat, light, smells. Sensory overload.

Here the crowds so dense progress is impossible, then a honking three-wheeler forces its way through. Baking flat breads, moulded on a rounded form, slapped inside the upright oven, scooped out and piled up to sell. Most stall holders Muslim, men with white skull caps, the women with scarves. The Middle East in the Far East. Here a Syrian restaurant, a Pakistani selling wooden spoons. Dates, so many varieties and qualities. The smoke from the fires, the cauldrons, the sweet makers twisting huge strands of dough as they walk backwards half way across the street, then turning and throwing it in a competitive dance for business, while their colleagues pound other ingredients with huge mallets. We can't get near enough to see what they are making.

125

Terracotta warriors and Xi'an day 2

The bus to the Terracotta warriors site leaves from the old city railway station. To get there we had to take the 601 bus. It arrives fortunately not full, but is high off the ground, with a further steep step inside. Here we find the first example of what becomes the Xi'an principle: stand still with a need for 30 seconds and someone will have figured out your need and how to help. I think people use that 30 seconds pondering whether an offer of help would be intrusive. There is an extraordinary, but concealed, awareness of others.

So we are helped to heave aboard.

At the station we are helped into the maelstrom.

Concrete bollards keep us out of the station as they are too close-set for the wheelchair to penetrate. Perambulating their perimeter we find one spot that has a lower, stone bollard and slightly wider spacing. We slip the wheelchair over and through.

The coach taking us to the Terracotta warriors was, like most coaches, strictly inaccessible but the driver jumped down from his seat grabbed my arms and helped me into the front seat. Personal helpfulness - but had he seen me while driving trying to cross the road he would doubtless have tried to mow me down.

The coach quickly fills and we're off, fighting for road space, cutting through bike lanes if wide enough, once even through a petrol station forecourt, when the traffic was solid.

The horn, that particular frequency that triggers my startle reflex, wielded as he tries to outwit, out-drive and scare everyone out of his rightful path.

I jumped so much I developed a stitch in my side and pain in my ribs and lower back. Finally, I turned up the volume on my MP3 player. So belated apologies to the people behind me who got Bob Marley at top volume. Well I am being the tourist today.

The journey goes on and on, the city endless, traffic horrendous. Then everything calms. We are at the edge of a flat plain and mountains are rising sheer and serrated just in front of us. We slow down to pick up more passengers, the bus scarcely halting so by the time those boarding see how crowded it is, they are too late to get off. We leave this quiet spot behind and plunge into yet more ugly urbanisation. The site itself when we finally reach it, after being hauled off the bus, past the endless street vendors, touts, guides, shops, restaurants, the endless tat that we hadn't expected around China's number two tourist destination, the site itself is delightful.

Pine, cedar, grass with a backdrop of spectacular mountains, the path winds up to huge stone built structures that roof over those burial pits so far excavated.

The crowds are rushed through in their groups and by staying still we gradually find ourselves at the front of the railings overlooking the pits. Peter starts drawing and disappears into a world of his own.

middle aged officer

Pit 1

129

cavalryman

133

The return coach trip, though the traffic was even worse, was less of an ordeal as the driver had a less shrilly pitched horn.

It was dark, near full moon when we got back to Xi'an station and the chaos here was much greater than before. We couldn't get on the pavement, let alone get near the mobbed bus stops. Any taxi that slowed down would have people opening the back door and pushing their way in. No way for us to compete. The hotel seemed unreachable.

But then one of those sudden shifts. A three-wheeler, auto rickshaw appeared next to us with a disabled logo painted on the side. We looked at this apparition and realised that it was the driver who was disabled. When he got out it was clear he had cerebral palsy. It affected his speech and gait, nevertheless he gave us a memorably toothy grin and helped me scramble in and haul the folded wheelchair onto the facing seat. We hoped we wouldn't lose bits of the wheelchair or ourselves as we racketed off down the road, along pavements - a rickshaw does not seemingly have to obey any rules of the road indeed it can go in the bus lane, off road, on a pavement, cut across side streets, the roar of the engine is in your head, a tune that is

on constant repeat, the rhythm leaves your body in perpetual motion, yet there is nothing as exhilarating making you realise car travel has been made so safe so dull, it is good to sometimes live life literally on the edge of your seat.

Xi'an day three: the kindness of strangers

Like anybody with a specialist interest, Peter always looks out for makers of calligraphy and art, and in one of the older lanes we found such an area.

The street was lined first with framers, then paintings and calligraphy, brush sellers, paper, inks. The brush sellers have large pieces of magic paper that show black when drawn on with water, fading as it dries.

He demonstrates a brush by drawing Chinese characters, Peter responds by sketching me, my face fading away before he completes it. Further on a crowd were gathered around a trestle- table.

A man was standing measuring out a long roll of paper which he folded carefully into sections vertically and horizontally like a map, leaving only part visible. Then his companion stood up and began gracefully, effortlessly writing, the characters flowing down the page. When he had filled a column, the other man would reveal the next section, blotting the last and the calligrapher would continue, the marvellous unhurried line, doing its elegant dance down the scroll.

Walking on, the midday sun full in our faces or clawing at our backs, we walk along the canal passing three young women deep in conversation under the protection of an umbrella.

Feeling hungry, we find a small cafe. We had just sat down when I felt I had to go to the toilet. There was one, up a stair and down a short but narrow passage. As usual here, the staff came immediately to help manoeuvre the chair, and when that got stuck, helped support me into the toilet. It was then I saw there

was no pedestal; it was a squat toilet. Peter and the chef between them managed to squeeze me into the space. He held me while Peter got into position, then discreetly held the outer door.

This is very illustrative of the kind of help we were everywhere offered in Xi'an. The meal was delicious. We came to a road that was only to be crossed by underpass. We assumed our walk was at an end when a woman pointed down the street. We carried on and the next underpass had, when more closely studied, a stairlift. Thirty seconds delay, then a young woman looks concerned and a man descends the stairs, looks at a notice, makes a phone call and waits. She comes up the stairs to gesture reassurance. Five minutes passes and a woman comes to operate the stairlift. Another small miracle: it works. A crowd has gathered to watch the unusual operation. Meanwhile the original man and woman seeing all in order have gone.

We passed the now familiar bakers and spicy tofu friers (delicious) with the wares sizzling away, a man in a workshop using a laser printer to create Chinese characters and ending our time in Xi'an eating the mutton soup traditional in Western China, watched over by a traditional scene depicted in blue porcelain on the cafe wall.

More than meals it was the people and their extraordinary levels of kindness that left me almost embarrassed they had given so much of themselves at no personal benefit or advantage and all I could say was thank you, about the only Chinese word I knew.

It felt inadequate but seemed to suffice.

Train to Shanghai

This afternoon we are on the next step of our adventure, overnight to Shanghai. A late checkout allows us a morning of exercises - I need to counter the effect of sitting so long by stretching my knees and hips[8]. At 2pm a phone call: time's up.

Can they book us a taxi? A bell hop hangs around outside for a while. No, it is difficult to get taxis at this time. Hurried consultation. The hotel tourist service can give us a driver for 100 yuan, about five times the taxi rate. We hand over the cash. He wants to drop us at the station perimeter. Small family groups are encamped throughout, eating, sleeping in the full roaring sun. We want our money's worth. A bit of sweat won't hurt him, rather the opposite; he doesn't have the slim figure usual here. So he takes our rucksack, slung over one shoulder to announce it is not his. He refuses to queue with the mobs besieging the ticket-checking hut, the first of the station's defences, and sets off around the perimeter to avoid it. High barriers all around. He negotiates with a soldier guarding a barrier to leave the rucksack, then back the way we'd come, enter the guarded area and back to claim the rucksack.

More negotiations and eventually we get to the next line of defence, the security check where we part. A long walk in the searing heat but at least he didn't have to wait in line. Narrow doors, the flow becomes more chaotic. Bags through the X-ray, the bag of food on my lap waved through when I mimic eating. Slightly calmer waters carry us towards the various waiting rooms. We need the one appropriate for our train. So many. The indicator boards flash destinations in Chinese but with numbers we can recognise. We make ourselves known to the person controlling the entrance to our hall and are waved to sit in a certain area. I carry on writing my blog offline. Well before time a young man appears and confusingly, leads us back, out of the station, all that hard won territory abandoned, back into the punishing light. Difficult to keep up with him through the crowds. Then back in through the exit gates and down a long rutted ramp leading to the depths beneath the station. We are pushing against the flow, the endless masses pouring down ramps off the arriving train. No indicators here. Our guide consults another. The flow slackens and we are going up to the platform. Our train. There is a very high step into it as the platform is so low. We now have a senior (and therefore rotund?) member of staff beside the thin young one. The platform is otherwise deserted. We continue standing there. Passengers start to arrive and are soon mobbing the train. We stay put and grow uneasy. Are they having trouble getting the ramp to let us board? Mr Chubby turns and talks to us at length, in Chinese. We shrug our total lack of understanding. He starts asking boarding passengers something, perhaps to swap berths with us? A woman turns to us. There is a disabled space at the other end of the train, room for the wheelchair, unlike here, but it is hard class, not the soft sleeper we have booked. He has been trying to find someone to translate to us. English is not widely understood.

Time is now short.

We move as fast as we can following Chubby through the crowds, right to the back of the train. Wheelchair lifted in. Wide space, like on the Trans Sib, WC next to our space, but there is no door to our space. The bunks are narrow, the "disabled" one is very low and there is a third bed high against the ceiling. A young couple are evicted from the lower bunks, the lowest of which has a sign in English and Chinese "reserved for disabled". There is a long three-way discussion between Chubby and the young woman. We assume they will take our soft beds in return. This for some reason turns out not to be possible. Her suitcase is moved and the wheelchair parked. She uses the small footholds to make the difficult ascent to her high perch and goes to sleep. The bed is very low and narrow and there is some very large sharp object under it. We are in full view of this much livelier end of the train. People perch on fold down seats in the corridor as the hard sleeper bunks don't allow sitting. They talk, eat - on all trains and every station there are sources of boiling water for tea and instant noodles which are sold everywhere - and play music on their smart phones. If the Trans Sib was isolation, this is immolation.

No door, so we are bathed in many conversations which, not understood, wash over us like soothing waves on a shore. Not so with the young man perched outside our space. His mobile held high plays French love songs at full volume, the known words forcing themselves into my brain. No one objects, except us under our breath. An older man insists on helping me into the toilet, out of it and safely back to the compartment. No sense of embarrassment that would be present at home. We haven't gone far when the train stops. Shortly after starting off we come to a sudden halt yet again. I lie down and am back in that lulled-train mode induced by the Trans Sib, back in a familiar environment. It is funny how quickly something so alien and full of potential pitfalls and worries can be like returning home.

6.30 am the conductor comes into our space and opens the curtains she had drawn the night before. I mentally check how my muscles are feeling. Since arriving in the heat my muscles have been relaxed and I've been virtually pain free.

We gather our belongings ready to get off for our scheduled 8am arrival.

Huge buildings signal Shanghai, but we're very puzzled to see the train plunge into fields again. Now we pull into a station: Nanjing. We are running late, hours away from Shanghai.

Great, it means we can spend the morning stretching out, rather than arriving at the hotel six hours before check-in. Coffee, dried bananas and peanuts.

Finally Shanghai. High platform, ramps, easy out. Now for a taxi. Problem. The taxi rank is underground, access via steep escalator, not possible for us.

We wander around the station to where the taxis plunge underground. A policeman there understands our problem, waves a taxi down before he takes the plunge and tells him to pick us up.

To the Bund and our stately old hotel.

Shanghai day one

The taxi drops us outside the hotel, stone, four or five storeys, European, mid 19th century, once imposing, now human among the gigantic towers.

It is listed as having facilities for the disabled. Two steps then another two into the lobby. The manager is there to oversee the help of a troop of bell hops.

After a night in hard sleeper our clothes are not of the newest and our rucksack looks distressed among the designer luggage. But we are checked in and head for the lift.

A restraining gesture. The lift is at the top of a thickly carpeted flight of stairs. Peter starts taking me in the chair backwards up them, step by step. He has a technique. The bell hops gather round needing to be seen to be useful. They lift the front of the chair, forcing Peter also to lift it, so directly taking almost all the weight. He can't get them to simply hold the front to steady his progress.

The room is spacious, has a lived-in feel from the well-polished floorboards, heavy drapes, but the bathroom has no rails to allow me to access the WC, there is inadequate room for the wheelchair. There is a shower - but it's in the bath which is inaccessible. After doing my stretches, descend as far as the lift goes, then bump the wheelchair down the stairs, back out into the heat and humidity. Over a small bridge and we are in the Bund, the river front area of hundred-year old buildings, the remains of the Western intrusion into a then inward-looking China.

The river is busy with shipping. Peter is plunged back into the Liverpool of his childhood.
I don't see the connection. It's the smell he says.

Even some of the buildings echo for him Liverpool's Pier Head.

Across the river a backdrop of bizarre shapes, towers of commerce. Tourists, overwhelmingly Chinese, with selfie sticks and V signs. We've seen few Westerners. Streets, some smart, western brands, then older shabbier; food outlets, cheap clothes, mobiles. Then a recreated "old area', modern brands in traditional looking buildings. Very clean. Not our goal. On to a working area, the economy not of the Porsche but the pavement, raw cuts of meat, slumped next to piles of purple radish, small tanks of water, turtles, crabs, fish, unaware of their approaching fates. I now understand M's remark that in London you weren't able to see your fish alive before eating it. A seller squatting on the pavement with gasping fish on damp paper.

A noodle shop, the noodles continuously extruded for the machine, the young man cuts off a bundle and hangs them out to dry.

In China you are told always to barter. Peter takes to this with enthusiasm, replacing his disintegrated belly bag and broken iPad cover with one disguised as the pocket Oxford Chinese English dictionary.

When travelling, we have also found two hazards, people trying to be helpful send us in the wrong direction and our inability to correctly pronounce place names. On hearing us mispronounce the street we were looking for, one man came loping after us. He gestured that he had called a friend on his mobile who could speak English. We must tell her where we wanted to go. We tried but couldn't understand her English any better than his Chinese. The call cut out.

Sometimes the relief you feel meeting helpfulness is in the ending of it.

Shanghai day two

Today we head off at random into this mammoth city. This is possible, the pavements are smooth, road crossings traffic- light controlled (though ignored by two wheelers and right- turning vehicles). Huge buildings, without scale or grace, concrete gods of commerce, but with that raw energy of New York. Grid pattern of streets. Do what you want if it pays. But Peter ponders this grid, perhaps it is the ancient Chinese system of four we saw in Xi'an. Maybe something else is alive here.

At lunch we were helped to order by a slender young man in a crisp white shirt and tie. He works in a nearby office and his lunch break didn't allow time for him to finish his food. We wondered about his life, perhaps living in one of the many thousands of near identical 30, 40 storey high rises, air conditioners but no window boxes, no greenery, crowded. A long work day, long commute. How is family life possible? Yet people seem sane.

Further on into an older area of low buildings, narrow alleys, communal taps, washing clothes in the street, public toilets. These areas are being eroded, crushed by the vastness around.

The wedding photos just off the Bund.

The old streets of low-rise buildings disappearing under the vast modern structures

The only graffiti we saw in China with beyond, scaffolding made of bamboo

Train to Suzhou

A friend, a Chinese acupuncturist, had become very excited at our proposed trip and suggested Suzhou as a break from the concrete-scape of Shanghai.

The air is thick, the dense high-rise towers disappearing into the murky concrete sky. Bus-boys hail us a taxi, explain our destination. There are three stations, the two new ones, distant, serve the new high-speed lines. Taxi meters are switched on when you set off, not as in London the moment they see you half way up the street. And for us getting in a car is a slow process.

The drivers have thick plastic shielding them from the passenger in the front. Communication is awkward. Elevated highways swoop and snake. We drive fast between the jams. Then the road is heading straight for an enormous glass dome, swings round it, stops.

Out of the taxi through a door into the dome that covers the South Station.

A huge structure, like a glass marquee held by 18 major ribs that branch into Y structures held by uprights. Minor ribs between braced by downward V s crossed with diagonals, form triangles and parallelograms of light.

Seen from the train: people working fragments of earth left among the pillars of new construction. Beautifully tended allotment, corn, bushes, veg, hens. Everywhere people sweeping, weeding, collecting used cardboard, drably dressed, almost invisible among the modernity.

A group of peasants, close together, in a field, squatting at their work, heads beneath wide straw hats.

Suzhou. A young student guides us up the long escalators to the taxi stand: the lifts are out of order.

We drive through streets lined by two or three storey buildings with pitched roofs. A calm, well-heeled look.

The hotel is in a large complex surrounded by gardens, grass, chunks of water carved limestone. It is wonderfully luxurious but most importantly, has the best thought out bathroom for wheelchair access I have ever encountered. I shower ecstatic.

Out on the streets, Cambridge comes to mind. Well-tended paths along canals, bikes everywhere. It is a University city and this central old area, delightful; though there is the usual vast urban area beyond, out of sight, the teeming tower blocks housing most of the six million inhabitants.

A narrow lane ends in an old humpback bridge, steep stone steps up and then down. Three lovely young women are watching me. I growled more to myself than anyone else, I'm not the local freak show.

Then I realised they wanted to carry me and wheelchair over the bridge. This doesn't happen every day, unfortunately.

Suzhou is famous as a centre for silk production. I had read of children being taught to care for their own silk worms, feeding them mulberry leaves bought with pocket money at the school gates.

Suzhou is also famous for its traditional gardens. There was one close to the hotel. We set off with a map in English that didn't seem to correspond to walked reality. Asking people was unfruitful as they couldn't understand our pronunciation or read our map. This was a general problem with tourist maps. If the map were in English we could understand it, but no one else could; and if in Chinese they could but we couldn't.

Eventually this lovely lady intuited our want and lead us through a maze of alleyways til eventually depositing us at the entrance.

We had imagined lawns and flower beds made Chinese by the addition of willow trees and a round bridge, a garden for recreation. The reality was very different.

A very complex series of spaces, each demanding contemplative silence, a mixture of geometric patterning counter posed with natural forms, of strange shaped stones, of water in slight movement or of a tree gnarled with age and chance. We are entranced and sit while the hours slip away.

views broken by complex geometric shapes

Later, after stretching back in the hotel, we go for a random wander. Away from the tourist areas, a park with a group sitting listening to two of their number playing long stringed instruments producing a delightfully ethereal sound. We converse through smiles. A great pleasure here, this exchanging of smiles, particularly when we share a parent's delight at their small child, something that has grown very awkward in England. We here haven't heard parents shrieking at their children, children whining at their parents. This conviviality we will miss.

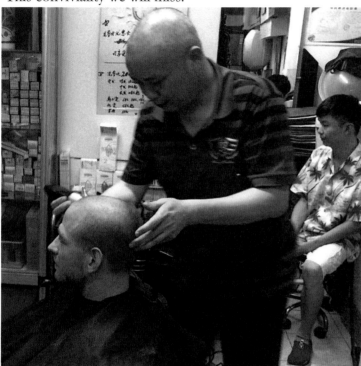

We pass a barbers and decide on impulse to get hair cuts. Peter indicates with his fingers the wanted length of his haircut to the middle aged barber. He is really delighted when he works out we are son and father, points to the young man on his mobile, who translates for us. They are father and son. A moment of revelation. The father son relation is highly valued, the general belief is that it is absent in the West and perhaps therefore the warmth we generally receive. They recognise a shared value.

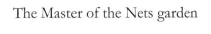

The Master of the Nets garden

Quick sketch of a brush painting in the Watching Pines and Appreciating Paintings Studio

The pool with tree reflection and floating petals

 On the train back to Shanghai a large group of middle-aged man, shouting jokes and anecdotes to each other across the carriage. Fuelled by drink? If so, the first we have noticed.

Back to the hotel the Internet connection drifts in and out of consciousness. It has been poor at all the hotels, only once strong enough to allow VPN access to Facebook (officially banned in China). Now I can't do email let alone upload my blog.

We eat in a local cafe, Muslim, people from China's north west. The young man serving has cerebral palsy. He walks with a loping gait, but doesn't spill a drop. We exchange glances, recognising shared experience. The women have headscarves. One kneels to pray in a narrow space between the tables.

Randomly wander on, we pause outside a motorcycle repair shop, not the common electric bikes, but the real beasts, Harley's.

The owner is in a mezzanine, playing pool by himself. Something keeps us there.

Then we remember. The right-hand brake is loose, needs an Allen key to tighten it. We have been asking at all the bike repair shops and all our hotels, but no one knows of such a tool. They try to bodge with screwdrivers. Worse than useless.

Peter draws a picture of a key and takes it up to the pool player. He comes to look, dives back into his workshop and returns with the real thing.

We put the success down to the random walk as well as the kindness of strangers.

Shanghai Museum

The humidity has reached 99%. For Peter every action is in slow motion, through a veil of sweat. Myself, I adore heat, my muscles relax, so I can sit for far longer periods in my wheelchair than I can in the U.K. Taxi to the Shanghai museum, a beautiful modern gallery, fully accessible, but with rather over enthusiastic air conditioning.

木石而無竹則黯然無
意在畫竹則竹為主以
也亦泥古法不執己覺惟在適

163

四時之吏五行之佐宣其氣美

After the chill of the gallery I would like to stretch. The hotel is too far so we improvise. There is a park, formal, grass for looking at, not touching, anyway damp after the overnight storm. The benches are divided into individual seats, so we try the low wall that edges the grass. Wheelchair seat and back support my head, my raincoat pads underneath.

Peter massages my legs to many interested and approving glances.

Back into a traditional area, part demolished. Men squat among the ruins buying and selling small song birds. Further in, down very narrow alleys with right angle turns, there are communal taps, women washing clothes at a washboard. We emerge on a lively street, the high rises edging in on it where a man tries to buy my wheelchair; he hasn't seen one with suspension before.

milk for wet pudding (ice)

15:15
Shanghai
1 September
2015

黄开锡

Kei Zu Whan

69   34

69 year old Kei Zu Wan asks Peter to draw him as we sit in the park

169   Shanghai Fuyou Road Mosque dating from the late Qing

the bird market

Catching the train to Kowloon

We have the room to checkout time, officially noon but we can stay til two. Train is at six. Peter moves reluctantly clutching his aching head. So stretching, packing, resting. The women keep opening the door

wanting to clean. So leave our room, into the double height hall, past the photographs of eminent guests, Bertrand Russell, Albert Einstein Ulysses S Grant, to the lift inserted in the embrace of the sweeping marble staircase. We bump down the last flight of stairs to reception.

The taxi ride reveals blue sky, white fluffy clouds over Shanghai for the first time.

Outside the station the driver negotiates with the policeman to drop us in the bus station at ground level, not in the underground taxi rank, from which the only way is escalator.

He is gentle not brutish in helping me out of the taxi. Must be a father.

Through ticket check, through security to a help area.

Forty five minutes before departure we are escorted by lift to another set of security scanners. As Hong Kong is a Special Administrative Region, with different entry requirements, Kowloon passengers have to pass through immigration, quarantine and customs here.

On to a long narrow holding area that rapidly fills with squabbling groups pushing huge suitcases. There is a much wider variety of facial features, hair colour and physique than we have become used to. Also the language sounds harsher. Cantonese? The crowd grows more restive, ready to break the defences.

The gates open and we struggle through to the platform. We reach our carriage alone: the scrum is perhaps for unreserved standing.

Wheel straight on the train and down the corridor. We reach the compartment in the wheelchair. Soft sleeper complete with lacy frills on the seat backs and silk covered clothes hangers.

A couple come in. They have the two top bunks. Space is quite tight. They disappear to talk with the conductor and reappear to say they are moving.

Language doesn't allow us to know why. We are dripping with sweat just sitting, but as the train moves off, the air conditioning kicks in. What bliss to lie watching block upon block of Shanghai high rises slip away behind. Food trolleys pass. Our compartment is in the middle of the carriage, but the wheelchair is stored at the end between carriages - it doesn't fit through our door. Negotiation with fellow passengers

required to walk to the toilet; so while not quite nil by mouth I am even less by mouth than seems usual on this trip. Wash with a cloth in the compartment, then lights off and fall asleep to that familiar gentle rocking.

Wake to a completely different landscape, one that matches my memories of Chinese landscape painting.
Conical hills, peasants in conical hats, vivid green foliage, bamboo, water.

Frequent tunnels through the rugged hills mist swirls around damp, wide rivers, banana tropical plants, gashes in the hillside show bright orange red earth bamboo.

It is pouring when we reach Guangzhou. Our platform is railed off from the other ones; on board we have all been through Chinese immigration (emigration?). This is another of China's mega cities.

Then slowly to Kowloon. The last station on our journey that started in London a month ago.

The Chinese seem to have inherited that sense of innate superiority that characterized Victorian Britain. A friend in London, though exiled here for the last 15 years, is always exasperated by the time taken to, say, build a hospital here (years or possibly decades) with the time taken in China (weeks), but doesn't see it has anything to do with freedom of expression.

My reveries are interrupted as we arrive at our last station, Kowloon. Confusingly for me, while we have entered the Hong Kong SRA (Special Administrative Region), Hong Kong proper, the island where it all began, is a ferry ride away. As it is an SRA, we have to fill in immigration forms and get used to a new currency, the HK dollar, not the Chinese Yuan Renminbi.

English is much more widely spoken here. There we encountered few who did, apart from a few students and a man in Suzhou who had spent 10 years in Middlesborough.

We are waiting for a taxi when two young women approach us smiling and interpret for us with the taxi driver in Cantonese. I am now very practised at getting in and out of taxis, usually estate cars like this, sliding on my stomach into the seat. The driver asks me if I am ok, I wave back, everything is fine. Unlike Shanghai, HK is hilly and always visible are steep hills covered in green.

The taxi drops us in what seems like an underground car park, but there in the half light is the entrance to our hotel. It is embedded in a multi-storey shopping centre, stacked like an enormous termite mound, coiling upwards. It lacks any pedestrian access to the outside.

View from the hotel looking towards the mountainous interior.

The hotel has a good Wi-Fi connection, unlike any we found in China. We can also access sites like Google and FB that seem to be blocked there. But the internet soon tires and we try to head out but there is no pedestrian access down the steep coiled road that the taxi brought us up. The pedestrian door from the hotel leads directly into the heart of the up-market shopping centre. Eventually we chance upon a bus and metro station embedded among the shops. And here is the great surprise; the metro system is fully accessible.

Metro to the bus station, then a high speed chase on a double deck bus up a succession of hairpin bends I try to hang on as I am thrown back and forth in the wheelchair space. A young man wordlessly walks over and stands close to my chair, holding it still. When we arrive he walks away as quietly.

We wander along paths that wind around the Peak; the heat and heavy smell of luscious foliage.

The attendants help us down the steps to the funicular for the ride back down the Peak.

We walk on past the cathedral with its William Morris stained glass that the occupying Japanese army used as an officers' club in 1941.

Then a very complicated route of lifts and overpasses across the highways to the Star ferry that Peter wanted to take as it reminded him of the Mersey ferry.

We find a previous refugee crisis remembered in posters on the walls of a pedestrian overpass.

上海: 戰時避風港
Shanghai: A Wartime Haven

上海：戰時避風港記錄了第二次世界大戰期間，猶太難民逃難受納粹佔領的歐洲，到上海避難的故事。當時大部分國家都拒絕收留猶太人，由於上海港口開放，該地在1933年至1941年間收容了逾17,000名猶太人。這次展覽記錄了當時大量猶太人擁到上海的歷史和他們活躍的文化生活，及後因被日軍侵佔，對他們的種種限制漸趨嚴厲。被隔絕在虹口區內人滿為患，猶太人還要面對飢餓、疾病、心理壓力等種種令人意志消磨的難題。在展示他們承受痛苦的同時，展覽亦講述了當時救援機構如何擔當不可或缺的角色，向這些逃到上海的猶太人提供人道援助，並記錄中國外交官何鳳山及日本外交官杉原千畝如何冒著生命危險，協助猶太人辦理從奧地利和立陶宛出境簽證的事蹟。身於上海的猶太人於1945年獲得解放後，隨即亦喪失國籍。羅蘭士‧嘉道理勳爵協助數以千名猶太人借道香港，安置於半島酒店。香港這個中途站令他們重拾自尊和燃起前往世界各地建立新生活的希望。

Hongkew, Source: Erica Lyons

Shanghai: A Wartime Haven tells the story of Jewish refugees who fled Nazi-occupied Europe and found refuge in Shanghai during World War II. While Jews were denied entry to most countries, Shanghai's open port enabled upwards of 17,000 Jewish refugees to immigrate to the city between 1933-1941. This exhibition documents their influx to the city, their vibrant cultural life, and later, the increasing restrictions imposed on them by occupying Japanese officials. Isolated and overcrowded in Shanghai's Hongkew District, Jews faced debilitating conditions—among them starvation, disease, and psychological duress. Parallel to their suffering, this exhibition chronicles the vital role relief agencies played in delivering humanitarian aid to Shanghai's Jews, as well as the noble actions of diplomats Ho Feng Shan from China and Japan's Chiune Sugihara, who risked their lives to grant Jews exit visas from Austria and Lithuania. When Shanghai's Jews were left stateless following liberation in 1945, Lord (Lawrence) Kadoorie and his brother Sir (Horace) Kadoorie assisted thousands in making their way to Hong Kong, providing many with shelter in The Peninsula Hotel. This stopover in Hong Kong restored a measure of dignity and possibility as they set out to rebuild their lives across the world.

香港猶太大屠殺及寬容中心特別鳴謝下列人士及團體，全賴他們的幫忙，展覽才得以順利舉行：
The Hong Kong Holocaust & Tolerance Centre is grateful to the following individuals and organisations,

One of the overpasses that weave through the buildings on each side of the road and sometimes are served by lifts and a lively street market in Kowloon near the hotel

Waiting for the lift out of the metro station

This picture deserves a page to itself as so much of our travel effort has gone into battling or avoiding stairs.

其他乘客
Others

先使用
iority

An American on his honeymoon kindly offers to take our picture

as we haven't yet managed the Chinese selfie style with obligatory V signs.

185

On our last day here we decide we can just fit in a trip to the beach before we have to make our way to the airport later that afternoon. So metro to Tin Hau station in Causeway Bay on the north side of HK island. Named after Tin Hau (Goddess of the sea) temple, which we enter by hauling the wheelchair up its steep stone steps.

Then through Victoria park, with its statue of Queen Victoria among its tropical lushness. We rest for a moment by a bench. There are two women softly talking together. I ask if they were on holiday. "No"; she is Filipino and I catch a weight of tired sadness. "We are nannies." She looked nervously at her watch. "We must go". We move on to catch the bus across the mountainous middle of the island to the south side and its many beaches. We are told of a beach with step free access and find ourselves in a piece of paradise.

People seem unsure how to use a beach.

They tend to stand fully clothed looking at the sea, not even paddling.

A delicious moment on the beach and then suddenly time speeds up as we wait for a bus back.

Eventually one stops and we set off on the wild ride to the metro and the hotel.

Quick checkout and I am doing our well-practised dive into a taxi. The driver is helpful as they all have been;

"The airport was opened after the handover. It used to be in Kowloon, you know, all those skyscrapers and mountains, the runway went out into Victoria Harbour. Tricky. The new one has been built on an artificial island with new roads, bridges, tunnels and railways. And of course they are building a bridge to Macao, the longest in the world, 34 miles."

He spoke with that pride in achievement that is common in China, despite the personal cost of much of the development.

Sleepless in Amman

Sandstorms veil the airport as lack of sleep veils our brains after a long crowded flight from Bangkok.

The last leg. Our last legs.

Hiatus at Heathrow

Land at last. Cramped limbs, sore bum, aching back.

Through the long flight, the longing for release grows so as the plane eases into its stand, the passengers erupt from their tombs like Stanley Spencer's vision of resurrection.

But for us resurrection is postponed.

My wheelchair cannot be found. It is supposed to greet me at the plane door.

The plane is now long emptied, apart from the crew who have to stay till resolution.

Two other parties are involved: the baggage handlers who are emptying the hold and the passenger assistance staff charged with transporting wheelchair users.

So a three way stand-off, the fingers of blame pointing in an endless circle. Voices rise.

Eventually the crew leave, the baggage handlers disappear and the assistance staff are left to find a chair to wheel us through in search of mine.

It is found folded on the floor near baggage reclaim.

Welcome home.

Endnotes

---

[1] Author of many wonderful travel books such as 'In Arabian Nights' and more recently a series of fantastic novels.
[2] https://www.bbc.co.uk/news/blogs-ouch-31923342
[3] We used the Real Russia travel agency to get visas for Belarus and Russia and crucially, to book a wheelchair space on the Trans Siberian. This proved difficult as the rail company required UK government documentation on my disability that we couldn't provide. We weren't sure we had a wheelchair accessible space on the train til we boarded.
[4] Though in the end the help never materialised.
[5] We have one change of clothes. They are suitable for warm dry weather and assume they can be washed and dry overnight. We also carry my splints. These are used to hold my knees in extension after my daily exercise routine. Rain we don't cater for.
[6] Perhaps I should say that I don't self propel my wheelchair except for short distances around a room.
[7] I have a very strong startle reflex. This is common in people with Cerebral Palsy. It means that sudden loud noises, particularly shrill ones like the barking of a dog, can cause whole body spasms (severe cramp) which are very painful.
[8] Joints such as knees and hips, if kept flexed (bent) in one position for too long, lose the ability to fully straighten. Hence the vital importance for wheelchair users to have physiotherapy. I have been receiving Bobath physio for most of my life.